Kid Care

by Laura Shallop
illustrated by Laura Jacobson

Harcourt

Orlando   Boston   Dallas   Chicago   San Diego

Visit *The Learning Site!*
www.harcourtschool.com

Every day your body is growing and changing. Each part of your body does many different jobs for you. All the parts work together as a team. From the top of your head to the tip of your toes, you're the captain of your body!

As the team captain, you need to take care of each part of your body. Here's how to keep them in good shape.

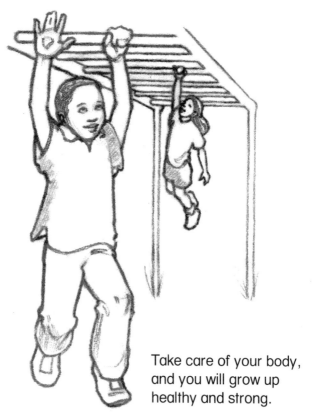

Take care of your body, and you will grow up healthy and strong.

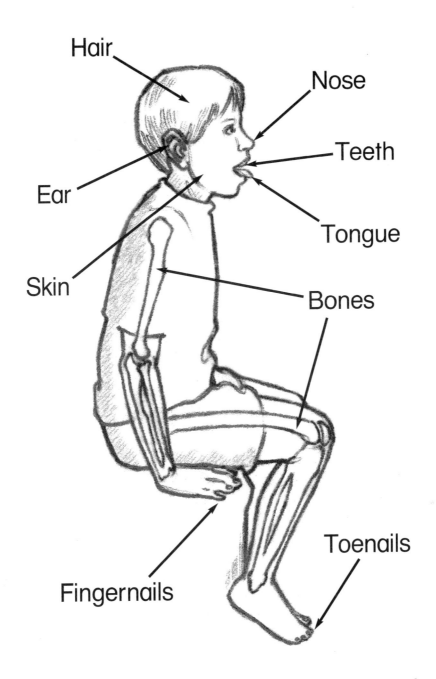

Hair

Nose

Teeth

Ear

Tongue

Skin

Bones

Fingernails

Toenails

3

Your Eyes

Your eyes are hard at work when you wake up. Your eyes are hard at work all day. They give you lots of information.

Did you know the eye does its own special cleaning job? It uses tears. Each time you close your eye, tears go to work. They wash away any dirt in your eye. Tears help keep your eyes clean and healthy.

Your eyes are very important! Protect them. Keep them safe. Wear sunglasses when you go out in the bright sun. And give your eyes lots of rest!

Take care of your eyes. Keep them healthy and strong.

Three Cheers for the Ears!

Sounds are everywhere. Your ears collect them. They help you hear chirping birds, your favorite music, and the alarm clock. "Beep, beep, beep! It's time to get up!"

When you pick up a ball, why don't you fall over? Your ears help you keep your balance.

Machine noises can hurt your hearing. Loud music can hurt your hearing. Make sure to wear ear covers around very loud noises. This way, your ears can always collect the wonderful sounds of life.

Take care of your ears. Keep them healthy and strong.

The Nose Knows

Noses come in many shapes and sizes. Your nose lets you breathe in the air you need. It lets you smell cookies in the oven. It lets you smell the gym bag full of dirty clothes!

Your nose can catch dust. Sneeze "A-CHOO!" and the dust blows away.

Your nose lets you smell the foods you eat. It helps you taste food, too. The next time you take some medicine that does not taste good, hold your nose. The taste won't be too bad.

The nose can let you know about danger. Do you smell smoke? Check for a fire. Does the food smell bad? Maybe it is not good to eat anymore. The nose really knows!

Take good care of your nose.

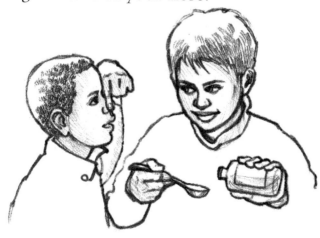

Straight Talk About Teeth

Do you remember the first time you lost a tooth? Was it harder to talk? That's because your teeth help you speak clearly.

Teeth come in different sizes for your growing mouth. They let you eat all different kinds of food. When you were five years old, you started losing your baby teeth. When you are eleven years old, you will have about 28 healthy adult teeth.

It's very important to brush your teeth after you eat. Brush your teeth before you go to sleep. Go to the dentist for a checkup. Keep that bright and beautiful smile!

Take care of your teeth. Keep them healthy and strong.

Your Tongue Works Hard

Your tongue does many jobs for you. It helps you taste and eat your food. It even helps you talk and sing. Your tongue helps you form different sounds and words.

Tongue, teeth, lips, and mouth all work together as a team.

Keep your tongue healthy. Brush your tongue when you brush your teeth. Don't eat foods that are too hot.

Your Bones

Bones give your body shape. Bones protect the organs inside your body.

Take good care of your bones. Wear helmets and other protection. Broken bones take a long time to heal. It is not very much fun to wait.

Take good care of your bones. Drink milk and eat foods like low-fat cheese. These are called dairy foods. They help bones grow strong.

Take good care of your bones. They will take good care of you.

Your Hair and Your Nails

Your hair and your nails are very important parts of your body. Hair keeps you warm or cool. It protects your skin, and more. Keep your hair fresh and shiny. Wash and brush it often. Wear your hair in a way that says, "This is me!"

Shiny hair also comes from the food you eat. A good diet works from the inside. It helps you have healthy hair on the outside.

Your nails are very important. They protect the tips of your fingers and toes. Nails help you hold something very small. Clean nails will keep your hands and feet looking great!

Take good care of your hair and your nails. They will take good care of you.

Your Skin

Skin does an important job. It helps you feel and touch the world around you. Skin helps you warm up when you're cold. Skin helps you cool off when you're hot.

Skin also protects your insides, so protect your skin. Take care of cuts right away. Clean them well. Stay away from the hot sun. Keep your skin covered. You can also protect your skin with sunscreen.

Skin likes a good washing, too! Use lots of soap and warm water. Wash all your skin, from your head to your toes. And even get under those fingernails.

Take good care of your skin. It will take good care of you!

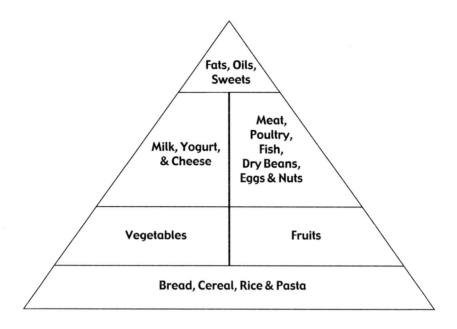

Fats, Oils, Sweets

Milk, Yogurt, & Cheese

Meat, Poultry, Fish, Dry Beans, Eggs & Nuts

Vegetables

Fruits

Bread, Cereal, Rice & Pasta

A Good Diet Counts!

The food pyramid shows the groups of foods that make up a healthy diet. It also shows how much food you need to eat. The foods at the bottom should be the biggest part of your diet. As you look up to the top, the amounts get smaller and smaller.

Your body needs energy to start each day. It needs energy to work and play all day. The energy you need comes from food. The most important foods for energy come from the bread, cereal, rice, and pasta group. You should eat more of these foods than any other foods.

Eating fruits and vegetables is also important. You should make a habit of eating them every-day. Make sure to choose different kinds of fruits and vegetables. When you add variety, you won't get tired of eating the same thing every day.

Other food groups are important. Foods such as cheese, fish, beans, and milk can be part of healthy eating. Most food from these groups tastes good and goes well with other foods. Grilled cheese sandwiches are fun to eat, and many people like them.

What you eat is very important. You should eat different foods every day. Variety is important, and trying new foods is important, too. Whatever you do, eat healthy foods. They will work for you.

Exercise Makes You Feel Good

Exercise can make you feel great. Exercise makes you breathe better. It brings more energy to your body. Exercise helps each part of your body get stronger and healthier!

Exercise with friends. You do not need special clothes or special equipment. You can ride your bike or skateboard, jump rope, or throw a ball. Sometimes when you play games with friends, you don't even realize you are exercising. Exercise should be fun, and you should feel good doing it.

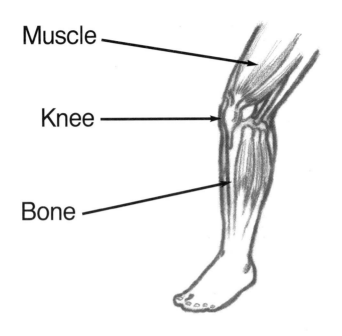

Muscle

Knee

Bone

To stay healthy, your muscles and bones need activity. They work together to keep your body doing the things you like to do. They grow stronger as you exercise. You should try to keep active as much as possible.

Regular exercise can help prevent injuries, too. This is most important when you are young, and your body is growing quickly.

Exercise every day. Find something fun to do, and make it part of your day. Take good care of your body, and it will take good care of you!

Why You Need Sleep

Everybody needs rest. Every part of your body needs rest. Most children between the ages of 5 and 12 sleep about 8 to 10 hours a night. Without enough rest, you may feel very tired.

Here are some sleep tips: Try to go to bed at the same time every night. Don't drink sodas after dinner. A warm bath helps many kids slow down before bedtime. Reading a good book is another way to slow down.

You are the captain of your growing body. Take good care of it, and it will take good care of you!